Healthy Me!

I EAT RIGHT!

By Kathleen Connors

Gareth Stevens
PUBLISHING

Please visit our website, www.garethstevens.com. For a free color catalog of all our high-quality books, call toll free 1-800-542-2595 or fax 1-877-542-2596.

Library of Congress Cataloging-in-Publication Data
Names: Connors, Kathleen, author.
Title: I eat right! / Kathleen Connors.
Description: New York : Gareth Stevens Publishing, [2023] | Series: Healthy me! | Includes index.
Identifiers: LCCN 2021037159 (print) | LCCN 2021037160 (ebook) | ISBN 9781538275368 (set) | ISBN 9781538275375 (library binding) | ISBN 9781538275351 (paperback) | ISBN 9781538275382 (ebook)
Subjects: LCSH: Children–Nutrition–Juvenile literature. | Health–Juvenile literature.
Classification: LCC RJ206 .C66 2023 (print) | LCC RJ206 (ebook) | DDC 613.2083–dc23
LC record available at https://lccn.loc.gov/2021037159
LC ebook record available at https://lccn.loc.gov/2021037160

First Edition

Published in 2023 by
Gareth Stevens Publishing
29 East 21st Street
New York, NY 10010

Editor: Kristen Nelson
Designer: Michael Flynn

Photo credits: Cover Maliutina Anna/Shutterstock.com; p. 1 Serenko Natalia/Shutterstock.com; p. 5 Oleksandra Naumenko/Shutterstock.com; p. 7 Rozochkalvn/Shutterstock.com; p. 9 aboikis/Shutterstock.com; pp. 11, 13 Gladskikh Tatiana/Shutterstock.com; p. 15 Stephen Cook Photography/Shutterstock.com; p. 17 New Africa/ Shutterstock.com; p. 19 StockImageFactory.com/Shutterstock.com; p. 21 Africa Studio/Shutterstock.com; p. 23 Drazen Zigic/Shutterstock.com.

Printed in the United States of America

CPSIA compliance information: Batch #CSGS23: For further information contact Gareth Stevens, New York, New York at 1-800-542-2595.

Contents

I eat many foods.
Some help me grow.
Some keep me healthy.

Carlos likes fruit.
He eats grapes!

Quinn eats vegetables.
She likes carrots.
They help her see well.

Margot is hungry.

She eats yogurt.
It keeps her full.

Rice and bread
are grains.
They give you energy.

Lamar eats a sandwich. Now he is ready to race!

Some foods
are fun!
Kelsey likes
birthday cake.

Miles likes to help
make meals.
He eats what he cooks.

Addy eats dinner
with her family.
They try new foods
together.

Words to Know

carrots

grapes

sandwich

Index